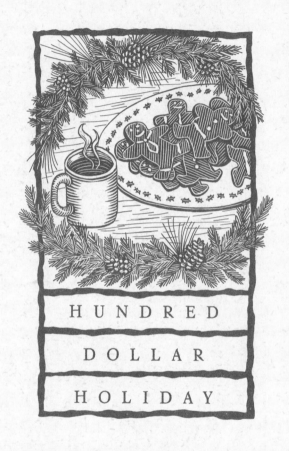

HUNDRED

DOLLAR

HOLIDAY

BILL McKIBBEN

❄

The Case

for a

More Joyful

Christmas

❄

Simon & Schuster

SIMON & SCHUSTER
Rockefeller Center
1230 Avenue of the Americas
New York, NY 10020

SIMON & SCHUSTER and colophon are registered trademarks
of Simon & Schuster Inc.

Designed by Bonni Leon-Berman
Illustrated by Dorothy Reinhardt

Manufactured in the United States of America

3   5   7   9   10   8   6   4   2

Library of Congress Cataloging-in-Publication Data
McKibben, Bill.
Hundred dollar holiday : the case for a more joyful
Christmas / Bill McKibben.
p.   cm.
1. Christmas—United States.   2. Simplicity—Religious
aspects—Christianity.   3. United States—Social life and
customs.   4. United States—Religious life and
customs.   I. Title.   II. Title: 100 dollar holiday
GT4986.A1M37   1998
394.2663'0973—dc21   98-41070   CIP
ISBN 0-684-85595-X

For Eleanor Kathryn McKibben,
on her first Christmas

Who Stole Christmas?

I'VE BEEN CALLED MY SHARE OF names, but the only one that ever really stung was "grinch." The year that a few friends and I started the Hundred Dollar Holiday program through our rural Methodist churches, several business-page columnists in the local papers leveled the G-word—we were dour do-gooders, they said, bent on taking the joy out of Christmas. And, frankly, their charges sounded plausible enough. After all, we were asking our families, our friends, and our church brethren to try and limit the amount of money they spend on the holiday to a hundred dollars—to celebrate the holiday with a seventh or an

eighth of the normal American materialism. There's no question that would mean fewer "Pop guns! And bicycles! Roller skates! Drums! Checkerboards! Tricycles! Popcorn! And plums!" Not to mention Playstations, Camcorders, Five Irons, and various Obsessions. Perhaps my heart was two sizes too small.

So it was with some trepidation that I carefully reread my daughter's well-worn copy of the Seuss classic, neatly shelved with *Green Eggs and Ham, Horton Hears a Who,* and all the other secular parables. There on the cover was the Grinch himself, red eyes gleaming malevolently as he plotted the sack of Whoville. He hated the noise of the kids with their toys, and he hated the feast of rare Who-roast-beast, and most of all he hated the singing. "Why, for fifty-three years I've put up with it now! I MUST stop this Christmas from coming! . . . But HOW?" Simple enough, of course. All he had to do was loot the town of its packages, tinsel, trees, food, even the logs in the fireplace. Even the crumbs for the mice disappeared back up the chimney.

But of course it didn't work. That Christmas morning, listening from his aerie for the wailing from Whoville below, the Grinch

heard instead the sound of singing. Christmas had come. "It came without ribbons! It came without tags! It came without packages, boxes, or bags!" After puzzling three hours till his puzzler was sore, the Grinch was forced to conclude that Christmas came from no store.

And so I breathed a sigh of real relief. Not only was I not a grinch trying to wreck the meaning of Christmas, it was abundantly clear who the grinches of our culture really are: those relentless commercial forces who have spent more than a century trying to convince us that Christmas does come from a store, or a catalogue, or a virtual mall on the Internet. Every day, but especially in the fall, they try their hardest to turn each Cindy Lou Who into a proper American consumer —try their best to make sure her Christmas revolves around Sony or Sega, Barbie or Elmo.

But Dr. Seuss's message went deeper for me. You see, when we'd begun thinking about Hundred Dollar Holidays, it was mostly out of concern for the environment or for poor people. Think of all that wrapping paper, we said, all those batteries, all that plastic. Think of all those needy people who could be helped if we donated our

money to them instead. Think of all those families who went deep into debt trying to have a "proper" Christmas.

All those issues are important, and I've spent much of my life writing about and working on them. But the more we progressed on our little campaign, traveling around our region having evening meetings at small rural churches like the one I attend, the more we came to understand why people were responding—indeed, why we had responded to the idea. It wasn't because we wanted a simpler Christmas at all. It was because we wanted a more joyous Christmas. We were feeling cheated—as if the season didn't bring with it the happiness we wanted. We were Christians, and we felt that the story of the birth of this small baby who would become our Savior, a story that should be full of giddy joy, could hardly break through to our hearts amid all the rush and fuss of the season. And many of our friends, Christian or not, felt that too much of the chance for family togetherness was being robbed by the pressures of Christmas busyness and the tensions of gift-giving.

Christmas had become something to endure at least as much as it had become something to enjoy—something to dread at least as much as something to look forward to.

Instead of an island of peace amid a busy life, it was an island of bustle. The people we were talking to wanted so much more out of Christmas: more music, more companionship, more contemplation, more time outdoors, more love. And they realized that to get it, they needed less of some other things: not so many gifts, not so many obligatory parties, not so much hustle.

Once, after an evening program filled with carol-singing and kids' stories and general proselytizing for the idea of simpler Christmases, one woman said to me: "Thank you for giving me permission to celebrate Christmas the way I've always wanted to." What she meant, I decided, was that the message from the pulpit allowed her to stand up to the pressures of the advertisers, of the glossy magazines with their endless decorating tips—to stand up to the voice that had been planted in the back of her head that told her what Christmas should be. What she meant, too, was that by giving her a target—a hundred dollar Christmas—our small campaign had provided her with an anchor to hold her fast amid the gale of holiday commercialism. There's nothing magic about a hundred dollars; truth be told, I chose the name because it sounded good with "holiday." And obviously big families

may decide to spend more at Christmas, and small ones may be happier spending less. But the hundred dollar goal seems to work well as a kind of check, a way of saying that your commitment to a better Christmas goes beyond merely complaining or telling yourself that this year it will be different.

None of this means that changing your Christmas patterns will be simple. It may cause tensions with other members of your extended family, or with kids who have

grown up thinking of Christmas morning as a lootfest. It may take you years to build down to a Hundred Dollar Holiday, years of talking and writing to your near and dear. In an obsessively commercial society, it will always seem a little odd to many.

But it will be worth it. I am writing this in April, and already I am looking forward to Christmas, secure in the knowledge that it really will be a time of calm and happiness, a season to linger in and not to "get through." A time to celebrate the birth of a Savior. This book offers plenty of practical ideas for new ways of celebrating. But it's as much a why-to book as a how-to book—it's my stab at a way to think about Christmas in our place and time. Christmas, this burst of light at the darkest season of the year, is too precious to surrender to the various grinches; it's time to build Whovilles in our families, our communities, and our nation.

Chapter One

CHRISTMAS

NEVER WAS

CHRISTMAS

This book, and the church-based campaign it grows out of, is not an exercise in nostalgia, a search for some perfect and uncorrupted Christmas in the past to which we can return. Christmas has been, and always will be, a product of its time, shaped to fit the particular needs of people, society, and faith in particular moments of history. And nowhere is that clearer than at the very beginning.

The Gospels offer no clues whatsoever to the date of Jesus' birth—not even to the season. And the earliest Christians worried little about such matters. Expecting an imminent Second Coming, they kept their hearts fixed firmly on the future. As the church aged and grew, however, some began to try and pinpoint the date of the Savior's birth. The guesses ranged all over the place, as Penne Restad points out in her *Christmas in America*. Clement, Bishop of Alexandra, chose November 18; Hippolytus declared that Christ

must have been born on a Wednesday, the same day God created the sun. Other authorities picked March 28 or April 19 or May 20. It was only in the fourth century that December 25 emerged as the date for the Feast of the Nativity—a date that on the old Julian calendar marked the winter solstice, the longest night of the year. It happened not because church leaders had unearthed some new clue, but because they needed to compete with the pagan celebrations that marked that dark season. Wild Saturnalia began on December 17 and continued through the first of January; the Emperor Aurelian declared that December 25 would in particular be observed as the feast of the Invincible Sun, the solar god Mithras. A couple of decades later, when the Emperor Constantine converted to Christianity, he built the Vatican atop the very hill where the Mithras cult worshipped the sun, and may himself have instituted the new holiday. In any event, veneration of the Sun was quite intentionally replaced by veneration of the Son.

And the switch certainly worked. Christmas spread around the Roman world (and into Scandinavia, where it combined with the Norse Yule feast). By the end of the thirteenth century, Restad notes, all of Europe

marked Jesus' birth. But success came at an ironic price. The old elements of the pagan midwinter rites never completely dropped away—the solemn celebration of the Nativity always overlay a foundation of revelry, abandon, blowout. And who could blame folk? The midwinter feast was a rational response to the lives they lived. As the preeminent Christmas historian Stephen Nissenbaum points out in *The Battle for Christmas*, December was a major "punctuation mark" in the agricultural calendar of the northern nations, the moment between gearing down from the harvest and gearing up for the planting. There was lots of meat from the just-slaughtered animals, and the wine and beer from that year's crop of grapes and grain had just fermented. In this life of extremely hard work and frugality, this season was the sole exception—there was no other time of year, for instance, to eat fresh beef and pork, since animals couldn't be killed till the weather was cold enough to keep the meat from rotting, and any meat that was going to be saved for later would have to be salted. "Little wonder, then," writes Nissenbaum, "that this was a time of celebratory excess."

The rowdiness took many forms. Strong drink fueled every kind of merrymaking—

using only the list provided by Puritan minister Cotton Mather, we find "Reveling, Dicing, Carding, Masking, and all Licentious Liberty." Men dressed as women and women as men; Christmas caroling often meant bawdy songs; as Nissenbaum points out, there were vast numbers of illegitimate births in September and October, clear evidence of the Christmas debauch of the year before. On these shores Christmas and rowdiness have been connected from the start. One eighteenth-century British traveler reported attending a ball in Alexandria, Virginia, where the elegant company stayed all night, "got drunk, and had a fight"; in the nineteenth century, great explosions and gunfire were popular frontier celebrations, with one Missouri lad remembering how he and his friends had saved all the hog bladders from the butchering, inflated them, and then "popped them with paddles" on Christmas Day. Even in the twentieth century we have the Christmas office party, perhaps our last link to those old celebrations (and appropriately enough, since the fast-paced and hierarchical life of the office is our last faint link to the brutally hard work of the medieval era).

The wild abandon of Christmastime led the Puritans to try and ban the celebration.

For a century in New England revelers faced a fine for "keeping Christmas" within the borders of the domain. But it wasn't just the boisterousness of Christmas celebrations that increasingly annoyed the "better class" of people throughout Christendom. As Nissenbaum points out, the revelry had a particular character: this was the one moment of the year when people who still lived in great poverty turned the tables on their feudal masters who usually dominated their lives. The various lords were expected to offer the fruits of the harvest to the peasants (i.e., to almost everyone), and the peasants were more than willing to show up and demand them. Thus began the tradition of wassailing —bands of boys and young men would walk into the halls of the rich to receive gifts of food, of drink, even of money. It was a sort of wild trick-or-treat. One wassail song went like this:

We've come here to claim our right . . .
And if you don't open up your door,
We'll lay you flat upon the floor.

But once the wassail bowl was safely in hand, the men and boys would drink to the health of their masters—in a way, the whole business helped legitimize the basically un-

fair life of a serf. It was, like the wild revelry, an understandable response to the life that people found themselves living—a chance for the powerless poor to blow off steam and for the rich to buy goodwill (and buy it cheaply). And if you make sure and leave the garbage man a Christmas tip, partly from sheer good cheer and partly so your cans won't be scattered across the lawn all year, then you hear a faint echo of this practice.

That kind of Christmas, however, depended on that kind of world—stratified by class but bound by geography and tradition. And as the economy changed, that world vanished. As cities grew and factories replaced farms, the powerful people in society no longer knew the mass of poorer men and women who worked for them, and so the custom of Christmas revelry grew increasingly threatening. It was one thing for your tipsy serfs to knock on the door demanding a roast beef dinner; it was another, as Nissenbaum points out, to have "bands of roaming young street toughs . . . traveling freely and menacing wherever they pleased." Instead of a pause in the agricultural cycle, these young men now often faced seasonal unemployment. Disguised, as in the old days of mumming, sometimes beating on drums and kettles, these gangs would invade the rich

districts of American cities and then sometimes head on to the black neighborhoods where they would trash churches and beat up passersby. The "beastly vice of drunkenness among the lower laboring classes is growing to a frightful excess," fretted an upper-class New Yorker in the early 1800s. "Thefts, incendiaries, and murders—which prevail—all arise from this source."

And so, more or less self-consciously, a group of upper-class New Yorkers set out to reinvent the holiday, an effort that proved to be of far more long-lasting importance than the earlier Puritan effort to stamp out the celebrations entirely. Washington Irving was one key figure; in 1820 he published to great acclaim his *Sketch Book,* which included Rip Van Winkle and the Legend of Sleepy Hollow, but also five Christmas stories. Set in an English manor, Bracebridge Hall, they nostalgically recalled the earlier agricultural Christmases with their roaring fires and horse-drawn carriages and tables groaning under the feast, which "brought the peasant and the peer together, and blended all ranks in one warm generous flow of joy and kindness." Popular as the stories were, however, as Nissenbaum points out, "Washington Irving's vision did not exactly offer a practical model for anyone who was tempted—and

many must have been—to celebrate Christmas in this fashion." The task of inventing a "traditional" Christmas more appropriate to modern lives was left to others, especially Clement Clark Moore.

Moore, an extremely rich professor of Hebrew, grew up on a rural estate called Chelsea. Present-day New Yorkers will know the spot as . . . Chelsea, the part of Manhattan that stretches from Nineteenth Street to Twenty-fourth Street and from Eighth Avenue to Tenth Avenue. Indeed, Ninth Avenue was dug smack through the middle of his estate in 1818, right about the time he was writing "A Visit from Saint Nicholas," which is the poem we know as "The Night Before Christmas." Moore did not take kindly to the changes going on around him; as Nissenbaum discovers, he believed that the city was being taken over by a conspiracy of "cartmen, carpenters, masons, pavers, and all their host of attendant laborers." And he feared that the mob would abolish all the old elite life of New York: "We know not the amount nor the extent of oppression which may yet be reserved for us." So it comes as no surprise that Moore didn't care for the character of urban Christmases. And in his beloved poem, he manages to offer an alter-

native—the figure of Santa Claus, of Saint Nick. Santa was distantly related, of course, to the Saint Nicholas born in third-century Turkey (a creature so pious that even as an infant he somehow knew to refrain from suckling his mother on fast days). By the Renaissance, says Restad, he had become "the favorite saint of nearly everyone." His good image survived even the Protestant reaction against saints, especially in Holland. And since Moore, a member of the New-York Historical Society, was interested in the city's early Dutch heritage, it's no wonder that that's where he, like Washington Irving before him, turned for his figure of Christmas.

But there was no Santa Claus tradition in this country—no reindeer, no sleigh, no coming-down-the-chimney—until Moore invented it. And, as Nissenbaum notes, what was most interesting about his invention was that Santa Claus was not an authority figure, not a bishop or a patriarch. Unlike the mitred and robed Saint Nicholas, he was just a right jolly old elf with twinkling eyes, rosy cheeks, and the famous shaking belly. Not only that, he looked "like a peddler just opening his pack"—that is, like a lower-class tradesman. And yet he invaded your home

not to cause trouble, demand food, and shake up the social order, but to leave presents! What a guy!

Better yet, even as the new Santa reversed one social order, he left another intact. Since parents had to buy and wrap the presents that Santa Claus supposedly delivered to their children, the old idea of Christmas as a time to take care of the weaker, the dependent, was preserved. Grown-ups could have their cake—the feeling of goodwill that comes with being a beneficent lord—and not have to worry that some ruffian was going to steal it. So Santa Claus, and the rituals of giving presents, served to bring Christmas inside the home where it was safe. Very slowly but surely, the Christmas chaos in the streets subsided, replaced by the happy riot of gifts inside. As Nissenbaum points out, "this is not to say that the rowdy Christmas season simply disappeared"; for decades, he discovers, the December newspapers were filled with reports of out-of-control street revels. But they also were crammed with editorials welcoming the season of peace. And the tide was running in the direction of the living room and away from the street. "Let all avoid taverns and grog shops for a few days at least, and spend their money at home," advised the *New York*

Herald in 1839. "Make glad upon one day the domestic hearth, the virtuous wife, the smiling, merry-hearted children, and the blessed mother." A new Christmas had been born, again appropriate to the needs of the day.

That new Christmas was greeted with the greatest enthusiasm by the emerging class of American entrepreneurs, who saw in it a source of vast potential wealth. Consider the story Restad tells of F. W. Woolworth, who one year allowed himself to be persuaded to stock some German-made glass Christmas ornaments at his small store. In two days they had all been sold, and Woolworth "woke up." He was soon making regular visits to Germany, and ordering fifteen hundred gross of ornaments at a time (and remarking idly on the poverty of the bauble-makers, who might command a wage of three dollars per week). By the end of the nineteenth century, his Christmas trade alone netted Woolworth half a million dollars. "This is our harvest time—make it pay," he instructed his managers. There was a similar boom in Christmas cards—at one time, writes Restad, the "top event" of the New York art season was an annual competition sponsored by the chief lithography company for the next year's card designs.

And of course there were the presents. Though historians can find newspaper ads for holiday gifts back nearly to 1800, the great boom followed this reinvention of the holiday as a family celebration. The department stores then emerging in the big cities started the custom of dressing their windows to attract the throngs of shoppers, who were now able to walk the streets without fear of reveling gangs. As early as 1867, Macy's was staying open till midnight on Christmas Eve. Bookstores sold enormous numbers of ornate "gift books" that publishers produced each fall. Toy stores, able to count on a guaranteed profitable season, began to spread across the land. Advertisers offered extensive catalogues of their wares—The Game of Pope and Pagan, The Game of Cup and Ball, Jack Straws, Dr. Busby's Cards; already the list was long enough to torture any child. As Nissenbaum points out, as early as 1845 there was even a children's game about the process of Christmas shopping itself, "the laughable game of 'What d'ye Buy.' " Special candies poured forth from the confectioners, special songs from the sheet music companies. In a way, writes Nissenbaum, the new celebration of Christmas served as a way to educate Americans, traditionally distrustful of luxury and excess, to the joys of buying

things they didn't strictly need. "It was the thin end of the wedge by which many Americans became enmeshed in the more self-indulgent aspects of consumer spending . . . a crucial means of legitimizing the penetration of consumerist behavior into American society."

But as might be expected, this new Christmas had no sooner solved one set of problems—rowdyism—than it began to be accused of creating another—selfishness. Almost from the start, many people worried at least a little that Christmas was getting out of hand. And almost from the start there were a few cranks and scolds, of which I suppose I must count myself as a contemporary version, who insisted loudly that the holiday was too commercial. Mostly, people worried that their children were being spoiled, that in Nissenbaum's words "the holiday season was an infectious breeding ground for juvenile materialism and greed." (He quotes from as early as 1829 a letter from a nine-year-old to her aunt expressing the hope "that Santa Claus has given you at least as many presents as he has me, for he only gave me four.")

And one of the responses to those fears, oddly enough, was the spread of the Christmas tree. When I was growing up in Lexing-

ton, Massachusetts, we always purchased our tree from the stand set up by the Follen Unitarian Church—a church named for the progressive scholar who helped introduce the custom of Christmas trees to the country. Karl Follen (who changed his name to Charles when he hit these shores) was exiled from Germany for liberal political activities. He was successful on his arrival, earning a professorship at Harvard in German literature, but again his politics plagued him—he was too radical an abolitionist for the proper Bostonians, and he lost his job. That very Christmas, however, a visiting British writer

and fellow abolitionist, Harriet Martineau, watched as he decorated his tree with dozens of wax candles and then, like a magician unhatting a rabbit, ushered in his son, Charley, and some friends. "Their faces were upturned to the blaze, all eyes wide open, all lips parted, all steps arrested. Nobody spoke, only Charley leaped for joy." She may not have actually seen the first American Christmas tree, but thanks to her widely read accounts, it became the first famous one.

And as Nissenbaum makes clear it was no accident that progressive Unitarians like Follen tried to spread the custom of the tree across the nation. The abolitionists weren't just interested in protecting slaves; they were also often particularly concerned with that other group of weak and defenseless Americans: children. They did not share the Puritan conviction that children were deeply stained at birth by original sin and needed to have their will broken. Instead, the Unitarians were convinced children should be trained to develop their wills, to become strong enough to resist their impulses. Unitarian parents didn't spank, they didn't scream. They combined love and moral instruction—and apparently no little guilt. The Christmas tree ritual, as it was prescribed by these men and women, was a way

to train their young. Instead of the old ways of getting presents (at the dinner table, or by rushing into a parents' bedroom early in the morning to demand a gift), the parents would now take total control of the process. They would set up the tree in a closed room, and arrange the presents beneath it, and finally spring the surprise, ushering in their offspring to see the glorious sight. Good children weren't supposed to demand presents; they were supposed to play "the passive role of silent, grateful recipients." They were learning "to control even their selfish expectations."

If this early instance of politically correct parenting sounds slightly bizarre, it clearly made little real difference to the culture of Christmas. Most American children were perfectly happy to add the blazing tree to the list of annual treats, and perfectly happy to be normal, slightly selfish human beings about the pile of packages beneath. More to the point, the Unitarians, and indeed the rich and the middle class, represented only a minority of Americans—most of our forebears were still spread out around the country's farms or packed into its city slums. While the literary classes were fretting about Christmas materialism, most Americans were still enjoying the holiday enormously

—enjoying, among other things, all the stuff. Indeed, Christmas was quickly becoming the one great American festival, the only holiday that was both religious and legal. Louisiana, in 1837, was the first state to declare Christmas a legal holiday; by 1860, fourteen more states from Maine to California had joined the list.

More and more the festival was national in character, gradually losing the distinctive touches that had marked a Pennsylvania German or a New York Dutch celebration. Thomas Nast began drawing the Santa Claus we know in the 1860s, and soon decided that his workshop was at the North Pole (before, he had rather mysteriously simply appeared in his sleigh). Elves followed, and Mrs. Santa Claus; Santa in a few short decades had become the center of the holiday (to the point, Restad reports, that one Pennsylvania father in 1893 actually decided to come down his own chimney dressed in red and surprise his children; stuck halfway down, he began to scream, which so frightened his family that they fled the home. Neighbors had to tear the chimney down to rescue him). Santa's canonization was complete by 1897 when the editor of the *New York Sun,* Frank Church, penned his famous letter to wee Virginia, who had written to ask if there

really was a jolly old man with a white beard and black boots who appeared to distribute toys. "Virginia, your little friends are wrong" when they doubt Santa, he wrote. Absent Santa, "there would be no childlike faith, no poetry, no romance to make tolerable this existence."

Christmas changed much less in the twentieth century than in the nineteenth—most of our rituals and customs still stem from the burst of invention in the decades either side of the Civil War. But the sheer scale of Christmas has grown enormously, as the advertisers and merchants have grown ever more adept at their marketing. Jo Robinson and Jean Coppock Staeheli speculate in their book, *Unplug the Christmas Machine,* that once U.S. factories had geared up for World War I, they feared peace would be followed by excess capacity. The newly developing art of advertising—the psychological insinuation that went well beyond the old listings of goods—helped insure that didn't happen; indeed during the 1920s the country went on an unprecedented binge of luxury consumption.

Ellis Gimbel organized the first Thanksgiving Day parade to promote his department store in 1920; Santa on a fire truck brought up the rear. Macy's started its com-

peting extravaganza four years later, all in an attempt to instill the idea of a Christmas shopping season that stretched from late November. So successful were they that, during the Depression, the big department store owners actually persuaded FDR to move Thanksgiving back a week to insure a month-long window for undistracted shopping. A Santa Claus school operated in the town of Santa Claus, Indiana, by the 1930s; soon its graduates formed the National Association of Professional Santas. If there was much danger that anyone would still be paying undue attention to the stable in Bethlehem, the media soon produced one new Christmas story after another, from Rudolph the Red-Nosed Reindeer (published by the Montgomery Ward department store) to Frosty the Snowman. By my childhood in the early 1970s there was an absolutely unvarying and ironclad lineup of Christmas TV specials, the syrupy scenes of the Charlie Brown gang, Bob Hope, John Denver, and dozens more all punctuated by Santa flying in and out atop a Norelco cordless shaver.

As I said before, grousing about Christmas is almost as old a tradition as celebrating it. Nissenbaum quotes the opening of a Christmas story that Harriet Beecher Stowe wrote in 1850: "Oh dear," moans one character.

"Christmas is coming in a fortnight, and I have got to think of presents for everybody! Dear me, it's so tedious! Everybody has got everything that can be thought of. . . . There are worlds of money wasted at this time of year, in getting things that nobody wants, and nobody cares for after they are got." By 1894, reports Restad, the editorialists of the *New York Tribune* were complaining that "the modern expansion of the custom of giving Christmas presents has done more than anything else to rob Christmas of its traditional joyousness. . . . Most people nowadays are so fagged out, physically and mentally, by the time Christmas Day arrives that they are in no condition to enjoy it. As soon as the Thanksgiving turkey is eaten, the great question of buying Christmas presents begins to take the terrifying shape it has come to assume in recent years. . . . The season of Christmas needs to be dematerialized."

That criticism, however, didn't strike very deep. For whatever reason, this newly invented, consumptive Christmas continued to serve the needs of Americans—probably because it was appropriate to a time of slowly growing wealth, and slowly increasing leisure. And it fit, roughly, with the various theologies of prosperity and success that dominated American Protestantism. The

cornucopia—the bottomless stocking—of the American Christmas was emblematic of our way of life. So for a long time, Christmas brought considerable joy to most people: one has only to read the accounts of prairie Christmases along the frontier, of Christmases in the encampments of our various bloody wars, of Christmases in the slave quarters of the old South, to understand the enduring power of the holiday. It's only in relatively modern times, I think, that the grumbling about Christmas has become less good-natured, only in recent years that significant numbers of people have begun to rather dread its approach. The spell cast in the mid-nineteenth century is wearing off, and it's time for a new burst of invention. That's what this book is about.

But as we consider new forms of celebrations, it's important to repeat one strand from this brief history: there's no uncorrupted celebration from some distant and pure time in the past that we can simply return to. Christmas has always been a concoction. So if we want to remake it in our image, we must first figure out what problems in our individual lives and in our society we might address by changing the ways we celebrate. We need to search ourselves for clues as to how we might remake this holiday.

Chapter Two

WHO ARE
WE
NOW?

The Christmas we now celebrate grew up at a time when Americans were mostly poor, mostly lived with extended families, mostly worked with their hands and backs. It's no wonder that piles of presents felt different, that rowdy noise sounded different. The Christmas that was invented in the 1840s was fairly flexible: people could change the size of their presents as the nation grew richer, for instance. But more and more that old Christmas finally feels played out. We've changed too much, and if we feel harassed by Christmas, that's why. It's not that Christmas has changed, it's that we have. We're like fifty-year-olds going to Daytona Beach for spring break. Maybe we can remember why it seemed fun once, but frankly we'd rather sleep at night.

But though we may not need the same things from Christmas, we still have needs. More needs than ever, in some ways. And figuring out those needs will help us to fig-

ure out new ways of celebrating. So the first, unavoidable, question is: Who are we? How are we different from the people of 1840, the people who were alive when the home-bound, gift-giving, child-centered Christmas settled across most of America?

That century and a half has been a time of nearly ceaseless change. Just think of the most obvious and simple demographic shifts. We live longer—twenty or thirty years longer than we used to. We've gone from a nation where the great majority of people lived on farms to a nation where most people live in suburbs, a category of place that hadn't even been invented in 1840. As a result, we've gone from people who did immense amounts of physical labor to people who do very little. The electric light has added several hours to the average day; we sleep far less than we used to. Instead of four or five brothers or sisters, most of us have one or none. There's an excellent chance we grew up in or preside over a household with only one parent; if both parents are on hand, chances are both of them are working outside the house. We can travel widely and easily; most likely we live somewhere distant from the place or places we grew up. We are entertained around the clock by images and sounds that appear from the ether. We

weigh more. We spend far more time in school, and far less time outdoors. Men and women have very different roles than they used to.

Each of these things, and a thousand more that we could list, have changed us. The world looks and feels different to us than it did to those five or six generations distant. That sounds trite, but it's important. *The world feels different to us.* Though we share the same biology, we're not precisely the same species that inhabited this nation in 1840. It's crucial to say, once more, that this is not a matter of better or worse. Life in the

1840s was not superior to the life we live, not purer or sweeter; perhaps there are things about it we would have been smart to retain, and certainly there is much in our way of life that those Americans would envy. This is not an exercise in nostalgia. It's an exercise in diagnosis. What are the problems peculiar to the moment that we might help ease by changing some of the ways we celebrate this greatest of national festivals?

Problems? Well, the environment, surely that's one. Our enormously increased populations and levels of consumption are filling the air with carbon dioxide, changing the very climate. I've spent my career dealing with these issues, and they are vital, urgent, critical, alarming. Name your adjective. But in a way these issues aren't fundamental. The damage we're doing to our atmosphere, our water, our forests stems from deeper dilemmas, I think—and so does the damage we're doing to the poorest people in our nation and around the world.

So the reason to change Christmas is not because it damages the earth around us, though surely it does. (Visit a landfill the week after Christmas.) The reason to change Christmas is not because it represents shameful excess in a world of poverty, though perhaps it does. The reason to

change Christmas—the reason it might be useful to change Christmas—is because it might help us get at some of the underlying discontent in our lives. Because it might help us see how to change every other day of the year, in ways that really would make our whole lives, and maybe our entire 365-days-a-year culture, healthier in the long run.

Who are we now? For one thing, we're a species hemmed in by stuff. The materialism of this culture has become a cliche; there's little need to repeat all the statistics and sermons. But just a little: the pollsters tell us that though we've more than doubled our material standard of living since 1957, fewer of us call ourselves happy. As a nation, we eat out constantly; we drink far more soda than tap water (and increasingly we buy our water in little bottles, because it's more convenient). The average size of our houses grows steadily—from 1,100 square feet in 1950 to 2,500 square feet by 2000. And we cram those houses with stuff, almost all of us. I think of myself as resolutely unmaterialist, and yet I spent part of this afternoon trying to wedge more books onto our already over-crowded shelves. It's not that I need them all;

I don't. It's that I acquire them, just like I acquire compact discs ("Eleven for the Price of One! And No Obligation!"). And of course our things need to be tended—to be cleaned, to be insured, to be safeguarded (Americans spend more on alarm systems each year than we pay in taxes to support the police).

I am writing this book in the spring of 1998, just as a new television program aimed at one-year-olds, *Teletubbies,* premieres on our public broadcasting system. Its characters are already being transformed into talking dolls, plastic figurines, jigsaw puzzles, pajamas, all aimed at "filling the one-to-two-year-old niche" in the market. "If this isn't the most important toy at Christmas this year, then something desperately wrong will have happened," said the man with the rights to all the Teletubbies products. Well, maybe. Or maybe something desperately wrong has already happened.

For the moment, forget the effect of all this stuff on the environment, though of course it's enormous. (According to the Worldwatch Institute, North Americans have used more natural resources since the end of World War II than all of humanity used in all the time before.) Forget all the figures about debt and bankruptcy and our general failure to save for our old age. Con-

sider only the effect of this stuff on us. Up to a certain point, it's delightful—we live in comfort, which is a new and still not widespread phenomenon. But past that point, and most of us are miles past it, there's something oppressive about our gear, our equipment, our trappings, our stuff. If nothing else, despite our ever larger houses we have no place to put it. I wager that behind the fixed grin with which we greet some grand Christmas present, many of us have thought: Where on earth is this going to go?

Here's the bottom line: we have so much stuff that a pile of presents is no longer exciting, no longer novel. How wonderful it must once have been! We've been reading Laura Ingalls Wilder with our daughter, sharing in the delight of her characters as they interrupt their materially bleak lives with a day of stick candy and rag dolls. But Beanie Babies arrive in our lives every week or two; kitchen counters are so crammed with appliances there's no room to chop and dice; a bottle of perfume lasts long enough that they pile up; even walk-in closets have grown crowded. When you have a lot of stuff, getting more of it is less exciting than when you have very little. That seems obvious—it's habituation. Hawaiians don't get so crazy excited about the sunshine; they enjoy it, but they go

about their lives. And we don't get so excited by stuff—or, rather, we do, but not for long. We've been so carefully trained to buy more that we find ourselves shopping when we're bored or depressed, but the lift from the new thing hardly lasts the drive home.

Even the strong beer, the rich food that once set Christmas apart now seem so familiar to us that it's a little boring; if there's anything different about the holidays, it's only that we break our various diets with less guilt. We eat rich food year-round; there's always freshly fermented beer; we don't need to beg the lord of the manor for a glass of wine. In fact, what's happened is that we've most of us managed to become lords of the manor, living relatively easy and abundant lives. We have sumptuous clothes, we have lots to eat. Since we live with relative abandon year-round, it's no wonder that the abandon of Christmas doesn't excite us as much as it did a medieval serf. We are— in nearly every sense of the word—stuffed. Saturated. Trying to cram in a little more on December 25 seems kind of pointless.

The materialism of our age may be the least of it, however—just the most obvious

and superficial symptom of our disquiet. Think now about those boys on the frontier celebrating Christmas by bursting pig's bladders or blowing up piles of gunpowder. Why did celebration mean noise to them? Most likely because life was pretty monotonous: week after week of hard work, varying by the season and probably rewarding in its way, but not exciting in the way we've come to understand the word. Not novel. If the circus came to town, that was the event of the summer, something to anticipate, savor, remember. But we have a circus of some sort every night—program after program rolls across our screens, each of them filled with explosions and shots, with hollers and screams. When we get in our cars, we reach for the radio dial as soon as we've turned on the ignition. Walk into a hotel room, and what is the first thing you do? Track down the remote?

When we occasionally think about all that noise, we're mostly concerned with the sheer ambient level of sound that surrounds us, a volume that increases each year. (The Noise Pollution Clearinghouse recently reported that when we raised the speed limit from fifty-five to sixty-five miles per hour, it was the noise equivalent of doubling the number of cars on the road.) But that's not

the real culprit. Much more, it's the way all the noises that we choose to listen to have infiltrated our minds. There's information in the very air, an endless stream of data and opinion and sitcom and commercial. I've taken long solo backpacking trips, and it's always been three or four days before the tide of CNN-NPR-Disney begins to fade away, before I can begin to hear my own thoughts. Before I calm down. Give us twenty-two minutes and we'll give you the world—but in any given twenty-four hours, we lack the silence and solitude to hear the low rumbling broadcast that comes all the time from your heart and head. That more important broadcast—the "who-am-I, what-makes-me-happy, what-do-I-really-want" broadcast—is too easily jammed by the clatter of our lives.

That's another reason, then, that our Christmas palls a little. The layer of excitement, of hubbub, that comes with the holidays now overlays an almost constant crescendo of excitement. (Every night on TV the anchorwoman sounds excited about something; every night she finds a fire or a murder or a war or a scandal to show us.) We go to the movie theater all the time, and watch ocean liners sink, starships explode; there's a much-hyped game on the tube

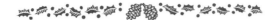

every weekend of every year. We visit theme parks and eat at theme restaurants and wander through malls and galerias and atriums designed to provide us with "shopping experiences." We're caffeinated, buzzed, wired, plugged-in. In one recent survey, only 19 percent of Americans said they wanted a "more exciting, faster-paced life." Excitement can't excite us anymore.

What can excite us—what can make us salivate the way a circus could make some Kansas farm boy salivate—is the prospect of peace and quiet. The prospect of a lull, an interlude. Stillness scares us (that's why the TV goes on when we walk in the hotel room) but it attracts us, too. If there's one thing we'd really like from Christmas, I think, it's a little of that "season of peace" that the greeting card writers are always promising. It's one of the reasons "Silent Night" is the all-time favorite carol. There's a moment when we sing it each year at the end of the Christmas Eve service, with the lights out and everyone holding a candle that frames their face with soft light, and that marks for me the absolute height of Christmas. When I was a boy, I never wanted to let go of that moment. I can remember walking my girlfriend home, and then walking two or three miles back to my house,

bundled against the cold, humming carols in the early morning stillness. It's not that this quiet is morally superior to noise; if I'd lived on the eighteenth-century prairie surrounded by windy quiet, I'm sure I'd have been out there blowing things up on Christmas Eve, and grinning as I did it. But we live here and now, amidst clamor. For us, what beckons is not the flash of the Saturnalia, but instead that little town of Bethlehem, with its deep and dreamless sleep, its silent stars floating by.

> *How silently, how silently, the wondrous gift*
> *is given;*
> *so God imparts to human hearts the blessings*
> *of his heaven.*
> *No ear may hear his coming, but in this*
> *world of sin,*
> *where meek souls will receive him, still the*
> *dear Christ enters in.*

We have other new needs now, too, beyond simply stilling the buzz of our lives, the chatter in our heads. We also have great need of time. We have come to consider it typical and unavoidable that we'll spend an hour or two each day commuting (nine

hours a week behind the wheel is the national average) to jobs where we'll spend ever more time (we work three hours more a week than we did in the 1960s). But while it may feel "normal" to us, it also feels grim: 69 percent of Americans would like to "slow down and live a more relaxed life," and 70 percent of those who make more than thirty thousand dollars a year would give up a day's pay each week for a day off work. What that means to me is simple: time is in many ways our most valued commodity. If we could buy more of it from some store, the line outside its door would stretch to the horizon.

Our strategy with Christmas, then, has gone slightly awry. We've gotten used to spending more money to make it special. But if money's no longer as valuable as time, we're offering each other a devalued currency. If you spend ten or twenty hours buying Christmas presents each year, you could use the same ten or twenty hours to make presents—time that you'd be able to spend with children, spouses, friends. There are lots of specific ideas in Chapter Three, but for now the general principle should suffice. If Christmas is going to be special, then make sure to spend time in special ways— make it relaxed time with the people who count in your life. And when time is your

most precious commodity, then the time spent making presents together is a gift in itself, and everyone around you will know it and appreciate it. The gift of time can come after Christmas, too. Many people I know give each other coupons good for a day at the museum, the zoo. Good for a backrub, even. The zoo, the museum, the massage don't really matter; what matters are the hours or even the minutes you spend together.

It's possible that you'll find yourself enjoying your Christmastime so much that you'll try to rearrange your life to have more of it all year round. Perhaps, like the hundreds of thousands of people who have in some measure joined the movement toward "voluntary simplicity," you'll decide to want less stuff so you can work fewer hours. But even if you don't—even if your finances or your psyche won't let you out of the race for very long—Christmas will still be an island of difference, a time apart.

A subversive question to ask yourself is: "What was I made for?" Evolution has equipped us with a grand assortment of limbs, muscles, and emotions, with a range

of powerful senses, and with a nifty intellect. And yet how much use do we make of these things in our daily lives? Surely we weren't born to recline on the couch, wrist outstretched, clicking?

One thing we were made for, doubtless, is contact with the natural world. How could it be otherwise? We evolved in close communion with all around us; our instincts, our reflexes, our emotions, our appetites, our sense of what's beautiful all draw from the experience of eons when we lived out of doors. (When doors did not exist.) Gradually, over the long course of human history, we've moved ever so slowly inside. But in the last century that process has speeded up —many of us have all but shut ourselves up within walls. We no longer need to grow crops, tend herds, or walk anywhere. It's entirely possible, if you command a parking space in an indoor garage, to go months on end without feeling the rain on your shoulders. We can live most of our lives at a steady seventy degrees if we choose, and many of us do; you can now turn your car on from the kitchen, so it will be toasty warm or nicely chilled by the time you climb inside. Even when we're outdoors we tend to wall ourselves off from the experience—count the number of joggers who are wearing

Walkmen and distant, dreamy expressions. And in the winter, in the northern climes anyway, we stay inside all the more.

But Christmas should be an invitation to be outdoors. Many of its symbols—the tree, the mistletoe, the Yule log—remind us of the pre-Christian roots of the holiday. The Gospel story, too, is filled with the flavors of the natural world. There's Mary, riding to Bethlehem on a donkey. There's the stable where Jesus is born, witnessed only by his parents and a crowd of animals. Some of the sweetest stories of Christmas concern those beasts. In the earliest traditions, the ox and

the ass bent low over his bed of straw, breathing through their great nostrils to warm him. In Spain, the midnight church service on Christmas Eve is known still as the Cockcrow Mass, from the legend that the rooster crowed *Christus natus est* at the moment of his birth. Across Europe, it was believed that animals could speak at the stroke of midnight on Christmas Eve, and Thomas Hardy, in a poem called "The Oxen," recalled the Dorsetshire tradition:

Christmas Eve, and twelve of the clock.
 'Now they are all on their knees,'
An elder said as we sat in a flock
 By the embers in hearthside ease.

We pictured the meek mild creatures where
 They dwelt in their strawy pen,
Nor did it occur to one of us there
 To doubt they were kneeling then.

Think, too, of the first to know the great news: those shepherds, camped in the cold tending their herds, and suddenly scared awake by the cosmic light show. And think of the Magi, journeying for months, eyes fixed on the constellations.

It took Saint Francis, the great nature

mystic of Christian tradition, to suggest a way to turn those stories into rituals, into celebrations. Animals, too, he urged, deserved to celebrate the great joy of this day. But how? He suggested that on Christmas everyone wander the fields and forests scattering grain and seed; that way the birds and beasts would have an easier time for a day—a day off from the hard work of finding food. And so now we do this in our family on Christmas morning, after we've opened our stockings and eaten our own breakfast, and it is a magnificent way to proclaim the good news of the day. If we did it every day, we'd tame the deer and birds, upset the workings of our small piece of God's earth. But on one day each year it is a mark of the bond we share with the rest of creation.

Human communities entice us, too, these days. As has been widely lamented, ours is not a great age for fellowship. By any measure, the level of participation in everything from politics to church to PTA has dropped in recent decades. A 1992 survey found that 72 percent of Americans didn't know their next-door neighbors. And yet we're clearly made for more contact with

the people around us. For most of human history, writes Paul Wachtel in his book *The Poverty of Affluence*, "people lived in tightly knit communities in which each individual had a specified place and in which there was a strong sense of shared fate. The sense of belonging, of being part of something larger than oneself, was an important source of comfort."

Now, most of us are so self-sufficient that we scarcely need our neighbors—given a credit card and a Yellow Pages we can take care of most of our physical needs. And we have a hundred reasons to keep to ourselves: we have no time, no one else has any time. If we do decide to go pay a call on a neighbor, the chances are good that the blue glow of the TV will be leaking out through the curtains, and that they won't turn it off when we come through the door.

Christmas, though, offers one of the rare chances to easily pierce those walls. The tradition of wassailing—of demanding a fine meal from the local gentry—has transformed itself into the gentler rituals of caroling, of visiting. It's the one time of year when with very little discomfort you can present yourself on the doorstep of a neighbor you barely know and hand them a plate of brownies. Our cookie route, over the

years, has grown to several dozen houses; there are a few people we see no other night of the entire year. But somehow that contact is enough to preserve at least tenuous bonds of community, to say "we're glad you're our neighbor."

And it's an easy time of year to enter the institutions of a community—churches, schools, nursing homes, hospitals. It's not that these places don't need visits and volunteers year-round (in fact, it's January when nursing homes get really lonely). But at Christmas it's easier for most of us to break the ice, for the rituals of the season are so familiar, so national. You know the words to the songs, you know the greetings and small gestures; there's something easy to talk about. Even awkward places—prisons, say, or mental institutions—are easier to visit for the first time at Christmas, song sheet or wreath or stocking in hand. Christmas is disarming. It's a time when, by mutual unspoken consent, we drop some of our various defenses, and so it offers, with its other gifts, some simple routes back into the community for people who have grown away from it.

Over the years, those community involvements may become some of the best parts of your holiday. My Christmas really begins

two Saturdays before the great day, when we have our Sunday School caroling party. We bundle the kids into cars, and drive from the house of one shut-in to the next, old friends that in the press of time we see far too infrequently. And then it's back to the sanctuary to warm up, drink cocoa, and put up the tree in the front near the altar. One of the older men has found it in his woods, cut it, carted it to the church. I borrow Bill Coulter's enormous wooden stepladder, and since I've got the longest arms it's my ritual duty to climb to the top step but one, and, leaning over precariously, nestle the star in place. And now, when I think of Christmas, the first image that flashes into my head is that ladder and that tall tree and that star. I wouldn't miss that day for anything.

There's one more item on my list of the things we were made for—less obvious, perhaps, and in some quarters more controversial. But I think we were made for some relationship with the divine, and I think Christmas offers one of the most comfortable ways to begin and renew that relationship, at least for those of us who have grown up in the Christian tradition.

Anthropologists, of course, have found the religious impulse in every society they've studied, and for a very long time Christendom was saturated with it. It was the air that medieval people breathed—their calendar was one long list of saint's days, and the cathedral the center of their cultural universe. On this continent, the Puritans woke and slept and woke again in a God-filled world; they hardly had need of Christmas as a reminder. But though we remain a religious nation, attending church and telling pollsters we believe in God, it's no longer such a natural and obvious part of our lives. Daily life has been secularized; we don't see the sacred in the working of the weather, in the rise of the moon.

The blame is usually laid at the feet of "humanists," of "atheists," of a godless intellectual elite disillusioned by the twentieth century. Or perhaps we think that science, with its wealth of explanations, has crowded out faith. But the more important answer, I'm convinced, has to do with the process of becoming consumers. As we've built our incredibly powerful consumer economy over the decades, we've been encouraged—subtly and not so subtly—to change the way we think. Once, working on a book, I watched every minute of TV that came across the

hundred channels of what was then the world's largest cable system on a single day. Those 2,400 hours of videotape yielded many insights, but if you distilled them down to a single idea, it would be this: You are the center of the world. You are the most important thing on earth, the heaviest object in the known universe. Each of your needs is of the utmost importance. Have It Your Way. This Bud's For You.

That notion, so central to a consumer society, is anathema to a religious one. Living a life of faith means, more than anything, putting something other than yourself at the center of your life. (Even for those who aren't religious, leading a mature life de-

mands finding some focus other than yourself.) The great and happy secret of every guru, from the Buddha through the Christ, is that when you place God, however defined, at the center of your existence, you will become more fulfilled, not less. (And conversely the great lie of the marketers is that the next treat you buy for yourself will finally make you happy.)

Christmas offers the best chance all year to see those two ways of life for what they are. We're encouraged to make Christmas about us—or, more accurately, encouraged to make Christmas about our children. We are encouraged to buy them stuff. But if we make that the center of the holiday, we help school them in the notion that transcendent joy comes from things. Since that's a lesson the TV tries to teach them every day of their lives, one more morning of it may not seem so bad. But Christmas somehow seems to make that consumption holy, sanctifies with its aura of angels and stars the worldview of the mall and the breathless catalogue. If, instead, you emphasize others—making presents with your kids, spreading seed to the birds and beasts, visiting the nursing home—it exposes them to the other truth, gives them some chance to see where real joy lies. As the father of a five-year-old, I'm

well aware that children aren't mature yet, that a certain selfishness is part of their nature. It would be useless and cruel to squelch that impulse. I'm not opposed to presents in the least—as you'll see in the next chapter, I love to make and give and get them. And I'm happy to buy them, too—my wife and I can make the hundred dollars our family spends fill a lot of stockings with funny stuff. The last thing I want is the kind of Christmas recommended by the early Christian father Gregory of Nazianzen: "Let us not adorn our streets, nor feed our eyes, nor gratify our ears with music, nor any of our senses, touching, tasting, smelling, not with any of those things that lead the way to vice and are the inlets of sin."

But I'm also unwilling to turn Christmas over to the forces of the secular world—to the people with something to sell. Christmas is too much fun for that. Some years ago, a wonderful Georgia-based group called Alternatives, which seeks to reform the way we celebrate everything from baptisms to funerals, put up a big poster that asked: "Whose Birthday Is It, Anyway?" Good question. This is a birthday party for a small child born to poor parents in an out-of-the-way place attended by cows and sheep. We know how to behave at birthday parties; we know

someone else is the center of attention, and that the pleasure comes from putting the spotlight on them. And yes, you get to eat cake, too, and ice cream, and maybe there's a little bag of treats to take home. But you're celebrating someone else. That's what the fun is all about.

And in this case, if you're a Christian, you're celebrating the birth of a Savior. So there's the absolute giddy joy that goes with the news of any birth, and also the solemn intuition that the chain of events leading to the first Easter and beyond is now underway. Like everyone else I've always loved Luke's version of the Nativity. And my favorite verse has always been the nineteenth, after all the accounts of angels and shepherds and swaddling clothes and good tidings of great joy. It says simply: "But Mary kept all these things, and pondered them in her heart." Christmas is a time for enormous celebration, but also a time for pondering, for reverence, for awe at our sheer good fortune that God sent his only child into our midst.

If there's one way in which the world has changed more than any other since 1840, one thing that's truly different in our lives,

it's that we've become such devout consumers. That consumption carries with it certain blessings (our lives are long and easy by any historical standard) and certain costs (first and foremost the damage it causes to the rest of creation). But the greatest cost may be the way it's changed us, the way it has managed to confuse us about what we really want from the world. We weren't built just for this life we find ourselves leading—we were built for silence and solitude, built for connection with each other and the natural world, built for so much more than we now settle for. Christmas is the moment to sense that, the moment to reach for the real joys.

Chapter Three

MAKING

MERRIER

There is no ideal Christmas; only the Christmas you decide to make as a reflection of your values, desires, affections, traditions. I have no ready-made set of directions for how to have a "proper" simple holiday, only the notion (that seems to have worked for many) that setting a limit on how much money you spend may help. And even that limit is more rhetorical than real—if it takes you two hundred dollars to celebrate Christmas the way it seems to you it should be celebrated, then that's fine. If you can do it on fifty dollars, that's fine, too (unless you're just being cheap). We keep rough track on the back of an envelope, but we don't worry about every last penny; if this is the year you need to buy some new wrapping paper instead of recycling last year's, no big deal. The limit is not supposed to hem you in. Just the opposite—the hope is that it will serve as a spur to your creativity.

If necessity is the mother of invention,

think of the hundred dollar goal as a way of creating some necessity in your life. Having lots of cash (or more likely lots of credit) may free you in certain ways, but it doesn't spark your ingenuity as much as a challenge, however artificial. The goal, however, is not to spend as little money as possible, or do as little environmental damage as possible, or any other worthy thing; it's to have as much fun as possible.

The very first steps toward a different kind of Christmas, though, may not be so much fun. That's because they'll likely involve explaining to others what you want to do. You may have to tell your parents or your grandparents, or harder still your children; you may have to write brothers and sisters, aunts and uncles. The best thing about the current American way of celebrating the holiday is that it calls together the members of our extended, far-flung families, and the last thing you want to do is alienate them.

So you may want to loan people your copy of this book as a way of trying to enlist them in your plans for a merrier Christmas; you may want to download "Christmas Gift Exemption Vouchers" from the Adbusters Web site, which exempts the recipient from buying you gifts conditional on them spend-

ing quality time with you instead. If they are likely to be lighthearted, you may want to send them the annual newsletter of SCROOGE, the Society to Curtail Ridiculous, Outrageous, and Ostentatious Gift Exchanges; if they're more solemn, the "alternative celebrations" catalogue from the Christian group Alternatives might be appropriate.*

Don't assume people will agree automatically with your plans; we are, after all, a culture that has been relentlessly schooled to commercialize the holiday. On the other hand, don't be paralyzed by the fear that they'll object. As we've seen, large majorities of Americans want simpler celebrations of the Nativity. Tell your family that you're not criticizing past celebrations, rejecting childhood memories, giving up on traditions. Tell them instead that Christmas means so much

* Adbusters can be found at www.Adbusters.org; SCROOGE is located at 1447 Westwood Road, Charlottesville, VA 22903; the address for Alternatives is P.O. Box 429, Ellenwood, GA 30049, and the phone number is 404-961-0102. Useful help can also be obtained from the Center for a New American Dream, the clearinghouse of the national movement toward simplicity. Call them at 301-891-3683, or write at 6930 Carroll Avenue, Suite 900, Takoma Park, MD.

to you that you want to make it as joyous as you possibly can.

Everyone knows how to buy perfume and neckties; if people worry about a transformed Christmas, it's often because they don't know what the new expectations will be. So when you talk with relatives, make sure you are free with suggestions about new kinds of gifts—everyone wants to give something. Tell grandparents that you'll tape them reading a storybook so your child will be able to hear them read it over and over; urge uncles and aunts to give a trip to the museum instead of a robot dinosaur. Don't be surprised if it takes a few years to readjust the holiday till you feel comfortable with it; there's no need to do it all the first December. Many families begin by drawing names each Christmastime, so that everyone has only one present to buy for the next year. Other families have developed elaborate running gags—in *Unplug the Christmas Machine,* Jo Robinson and Jean Coppock Staeheli describe a clan that each year passes around the same garish necktie, but always disguised (one year it was baked into a Christmas cake).

In most of the families I've talked with, though, people have come to love making some of their own presents for friends and relatives. And there's a good reason for that. In Chapter Two, I listed some of the things we were built for. Solitude, contact with nature and with our neighbors, communion with the divine, and so on. You could add creativity to that list, I think; after all, it was our opposable thumb, our tool-making ability, that supposedly made us who we are. Fewer and fewer of us do much work with

our hands, though; every year the ranks of the crocheters and the woodworkers thin a little further, and the children who grew up Nintendoing instead find it hard to imagine they could ever learn a craft, much less an art.

But here again Christmas can come to the rescue. No one expects you to build them a gorgeous bookshelf or knit them an evening dress. People will be delighted with the simple, fun gifts that anyone can make. And when I say anyone, I know what I'm talking about; after failing junior high woodshop and metal shop in straight semesters, I pretty much resigned myself to buying. But as we started this project a decade ago, I realized I did have some skills that might be turned into gifts. I could cook, for instance, and so I got down to figuring out what beyond cookies and fruitcake might make good gifts. One year it was bagels—which turn out to be simple to make, a dozen at a time, with a mixer and a kettle of boiling water. Studded with cranberries and frozen for later toasting, they made a great present, one that people actually used. The next year it was spicy chicken sausage for the many people I know who don't eat much red meat. All went well until it came time to fill the casings; the KitchenAid motor must have been

on a bit too fast, because before I knew it my brother was racing across the kitchen trying to keep up with a five-foot link.

I've made things you can't eat, too. Walking sticks, one year—I can still remember the pleasure of scouting for the saplings, of shaving the bark from the staff but leaving it on the handle, of coating the whole thing with clear varnish. They were beautiful; my parents still use theirs, and my daughter's, which was barely a foot long, always takes us back to that first infant Christmas. This year I'm working on soap—I had to buy a new Tupperware container to use as a mold, and a jug of lye, but I'm reasonably confident of success, and absolutely certain I'll enjoy trying.

My friend Celine Larkin is both handier and more organized. Each year she and her kids gear up a miniature production line for some gift or another. "I've been doing this for so long I hope I can remember all the things I've made," she says. "I started with dried apple dolls, then puppets, etched glassware, marbled fabric ties, and photo albums. Jewelry has been a favorite over the years. I have made button covers, cuff links, and beads, necklaces from found objects and fishing tackle." My daughter wears one of her Heavenly Hats, a beret sewn from polar

fleece. Last year it was homemade lip balm and body lotion. "By far the most work was truffles," she reports.

Each year my mother makes calendars for everyone in the family, each month featuring a snapshot she's taken. And then there's my favorite present, the one thing my wife, Sue, always gives me. She draws a picture on a circle of white paper, and mails it off to a Texas company that, for fifteen dollars, turns it into a plastic plate. Each one shows in cartoon form the highlights of the year just past, and now that we have eight or nine of them, every dinner can become an exercise in nostalgia: there's my daughter Sophie's birth, there's the new puppy, there's the trip to Alaska. That's usually my only "real" present, and all year I look forward to it, wondering if each small event of our lives will "make the plate."

One of our best friends cut and sanded some hardwood blocks for Sophie when she was two—ever since they've been the "Nick blocks." Her godmother, Shawn, and her godsisters, Annie and Nora, made her an alphabet book one year, twisting their bodies into the shape of each letter and then taking photographs. One year my mother wrote out all my grandmother's favorite recipes in a book. If there's a musician in your family,

have them record a tape—or maybe grand-parents singing the songs you loved when you were young, so that your children can go to bed hearing them as well. You can make a card game of family trivia, or pass along a piece of jewelry that has some important connection—small children will take quite seriously the idea that Grandma wore this brooch at her wedding, or that this was the baseball glove Grandpa used in high school. Instead of buying new ornaments for the tree, you can use old toys as decorations, each one bringing back memories.

And of course you don't need to give stuff. Gifts of time are often even better. A coupon for a monthly backrub, a gift certificate entitling the bearer to a trip to the zoo, a walk in the woods, a game of Scrabble on demand. Baby-sitting, pet-sitting, house-painting, bread-making, book-reading: there are a thousand things you can give to someone, and they will understand that it is really time you are offering. And since they know, too, that time is now our most precious commodity, they'll be moved. Many people love getting gifts indirectly. One year, for instance, our small Sunday School decided it wanted to support the Heifer Project, an international organization that buys livestock for peasants. The kids spent many Sundays

drawing beautiful cards, and parishioners who made contributions to the project got the cards sent to their friends and relatives announcing that a gift had been made in their name. We raised five thousand dollars, which astounded us. Even better, the combination of such a useful gift and such whimsical handmade cards seemed to please everyone; the next year we noticed that some of our friends had started to give the same kinds of presents in response.

I can remember almost every present that someone's made for me since we started doing these Hundred Dollar Holidays. And that's testimony in itself—I have no idea what gifts came in all those great piles under the tree in previous years. They didn't attach themselves to particular faces, particular memories. So the point is not to stop giving; the point is to give things that matter. Give things that are rare—time, attention, memory, whimsy. We run short on these things in our lives, even as we have an endless supply of software, hardware, ready-to-wear.

In the midst of this practical discussion, a practical question might nag at you: won't the economy suffer if we don't keep on buy-

ing stuff at our normal pace? It's a natural question, especially since the papers and the TV each year cover "the Christmas shopping season" as if it was the main drama of the holiday. The week before Thanksgiving is filled with "retail forecasts" from pollsters who have done in-depth research on how much people are planning to spend, and the day after Thanksgiving invariably features live reports from suburban shopping malls and downtown street corners. The returns from the crucial first weekend of shopping are watched with vigilance—are "same store sales" up as much as anticipated? Are retailers having to discount in order to lure customers? The coverage continues right through the holiday, with careful tallies of how many people are lining up to return merchandise.

There's never any doubt, listening to the reports, that we should be rooting for more Christmas spending. Consider the lead article in the *New York Times* on the day after Christmas last year, an article featured above stories on Mexican massacres and African coups. "Sales Disappoint for the Holidays," writes correspondent Jennifer Steinhauer. It's not that sales were down—just that they were only up by 2 or 3 percent. These "lackluster," "tepid," "harsh" numbers, this

"slump in holiday shopping," is described with gravity befitting at least a minor war. "Small, ominous symbols of the season's sluggishness were everywhere," reports Steinhauer. "CompUSA was handing out free videocassette recorders with computer purchases."

Such coverage could convince you that making calendars and giving backrubs as Christmas presents might damage the entire economy. But if you think about it, that fear doesn't make much sense. It's not as if the money you would have spent on motorized spice racks or titanium sand wedges is simply disappearing. Perhaps it's going to some person or institution who really needs it—a homeless shelter, say, where it will be used to buy food and bedding and soap. A hundred dollars spent on soup for hungry people goes into the economy as surely as a hundred dollars spent on Sport Utility Vehicle Barbie. Or perhaps you're simply squirreling it away in the bank—which is precisely what economists are always telling us we need to do in order to boost productivity and reverse our lagging savings rate. Market capitalism, if it is as rational as its proponents always insist, cannot actually depend for its strength on the absurdly lavish celebration of the birth

of a man who told us to give away every-thing that we have.

But if the economy won't tank, that doesn't mean some people won't be hurt. There are plenty of small retailers who do much of their business in November and De-cember—booksellers, small craft stores, and so on. We always couple our Hundred Dol-lar Holiday campaign with a reminder that people should shop locally for the things they will buy. And not just at Christmas, but all year round. To the extent that we're able to help nurture people's sense of community, in the end it will help precisely those book-stores where the owner knows your name, the craft cooperatives where you can visit the potter who made your bowl. Change in Christmas traditions will come slowly enough that most retailers will be able to adapt, just as they've adapted to a thousand other changes in our habits and technol-ogies.

And in the end, it would be nice if this revitalized celebration *did* affect our econ-omy. As Stephen Nissenbaum points out in his history of the celebration, "the domestic Christmas was itself a force in the spread of consumer capitalism." It helped accustom Americans to luxury, to spending on them-

selves. A more joyous Christmas that almost by accident consumed less might help slowly spread an alternative idea of how we want to live—it might help to baptize and sanctify the ideas of giving time and attention and love as effectively as the old-style Christmas baptized and sanctified the idea of giving stuff. It might slowly change the way we think about what we want and value the rest of the year.

People always complain that Christmas starts too soon—that the tinsel is up in the stores right after Halloween, and the carols gurgling over the loudspeakers in every aisle. And there's a certain truth to that, of course. But a bigger problem, I think, is that Christmas doesn't last long enough. One reason we all find Christmas so crazy-making is the sudden sense of anticlimax that can seize you once all the presents are unwrapped.

It doesn't need to be that way, not if you don't concentrate on the presents as the main joy of the whole season. We view, as I've said, the weeks before Christmas as the shopping season, but we don't need to. The church offers the deep alternative of Advent, the time of preparation that begins on the

Sunday nearest November 30 and includes the four Sundays before Christmas. The stories of Advent are powerful—especially the Annunciation, with Mary learning the knee-buckling news that she is to bear the Christ child. And the traditions of Advent can be powerful, too: walking out into the longer and longer nights, feeling the darkness that comes before the light of Christmas. At home, with children, opening the windows of the Advent calendar, reminding each other what it is you're counting down to. Traditionally Advent was a time of solemn repentance, like Lent; few people observe it in quite that sense anymore, but it can be a season of expectation, of yearning. At church we put off singing Christmas carols until Christmas comes, and instead for four weeks we sing that great Advent anthem:

O come, O come Emmanuel
And ransom captive Israel
That mourns in lonely exile here
Until the son of God appears

The anticipation can be almost ecstatic, the anticipation almost physical. In her remarkable book *To Dance with God: Family Ritual and Community Celebration,* Gertrud Mueller Nelson writes: "During Advent, we

are invited to be vulnerable to our longing and open to our hope. Like the pregnant mother who counts the days till her labor and prepares little things for the child on the way, we count the days and increase the light as we light our candles and prepare our gifts."

So Advent, though reflective, is not long-faced. It's filled with preparation, with plans. Not shopping—there's little need to drive to the mall for a Hundred Dollar Holiday. But present-making, and popcorn-stringing, and cookie-delivering; kids love sneaking off through the night to leave boxes of brownies unnoticed on front stoops. At our house everything builds toward the day before Christmas, when we trudge off in our snowshoes to cut the tree from the woods. Great debate ensues—we climb one ridge and then another, looking for the perfect splay of branches, debating whether the weak side of the tree can be hidden in the corner by the couch. And then we come in, and break out the old ornaments, and renew the old quarrel about tinsel: Is it ugly? (Yes.) And these ritual arguments are as fond as any other part of the celebration.

At our house Christmas Eve means two trips to church. One for the early service, where the Sunday School puts on its Christ-

mas pageant, a bedlam of wise men in bath-
robes and shepherds carrying hockey sticks.
(We've always been working on the show
for months, and like a good wedding it is
invariably marked by one memorable inci-
dent—the year three-year-old Lucas carefully knocked over the sheep with his crook,
say.) Home for candlelit supper, and then
back to church for the glory of the midnight
service, and the tolling bell to share the news
that once more Christ is born. Since we live
in the lofty Adirondacks, we all march out
of church singing "Go Tell It on the Moun-
tain." And the next morning, as I've described, some of us do just that, setting out
seed and bread for the animals as Saint

Francis prescribed, so they can celebrate as well.

Food, of course, takes up much of the day. If there are other people in your neighborhood or your church who are celebrating simpler holidays, invite them over for a festive breakfast at the time when you would both otherwise be opening presents. Making Christmas dinner is always great fun—too much fun to be left to the women while the men calcify in front of the tube. Everyone, youngest to oldest, needs to make a special course of their own, so they have something to boast about during the meal. We have a dear friend who arrives each year bearing two pies, each so beautiful that for a few seconds we contemplate not eating them at all.

And then let the celebration continue for days to come. The day after, host a leftover party for friends and neighbors—sample nine kinds of cranberry sauce. Build bonfires at night if you live where that's a possibility; sponsor hockey games on the local pond if you live where the water freezes. And so on for as long as you want. Light candles night after night if you can—candles are important. Gertrud Mueller Nelson's family celebrates all the feast days of the Christmas season: the Feast of Saint Stephen, Saint

John's Day, the Feast of the Holy Innocents. Like many Christians, they keep celebrating right through Epiphany, twelve days after Christmas, the day the Magi arrived in Bethlehem with their presents (and the day that the Eastern Orthodox still reserve for presents and feasting). "School usually reconvenes at about this time and it is difficult to slip back into 'ordinary time' after our extraordinary celebrations," she writes. "So it is a great comfort to have a final and culminating party." The point is to squeeze out all the pleasure and meaning, and to avoid as much of the exhaustion, as you can.

And if you don't have time to do it all, don't. Granted, you'll have saved hours shopping, looking for parking spaces, returning things that don't fit, wrapping piles of presents, making little lists, and generally worrying. You'll have more time than usual. Still, you should pick and choose. Just make sure that the things you do decide on are really special, really memorable.

I know that much of what I've written sounds like a very typical Christmas—and that's precisely my point. Trimming the tree, eating the turkey, opening the stockings,

singing the carols: if these things bring you joy, and for most people they do, then they are parts of Christmas you want to focus on. And you can focus on them more easily, as well as incorporate all sorts of new and borrowed rituals, once you've put aside the burden of buying carloads of presents, once you've ended some of your worries about what the materialism of the season means to your kids.

Most likely you will have other fantasies, other dreams—maybe a camping trip into the winter woods, so that your family can welcome Christmas all by yourselves; maybe Christmas afternoon at a homeless shelter fixing dinner. Don't do anything that isn't fun—at least, don't do it twice. If you go to the nursing home and it just depresses you, then save that for another time of year. The point is not to do good, the point is not to save money.

The point is to emerge from Christmas relaxed, contented, happy to have kept this season. To emerge closer to your family than you were when Advent began. To emerge with some real sense that Christ has come into your world.

ACKNOWLEDGMENTS

This book grows out of a project that I began almost a decade ago with the help of a few friends in the Troy Conference of the United Methodist Church, a conference that covers Albany and the Adirondacks in New York State as well as all of Vermont. I am grateful to the bishop, the administrators, all the pastors and laypeople of the conference. And I am especially thankful for Sabine O'Hara and Carol Anne Grieg, who worked closely with me on the first round of church meetings, and who each served as fine role models for the work.

Many others have been extremely helpful. The Association for Religion and Intellectual Life offered me a Coolidge Fellowship one summer to research the background of

Acknowledgments

Christmas. My pastors, Barb Lemmel and Mitch Hay, have been supportive contributors in so many ways; if they could somehow fill every pulpit in America, Christmas would be different and so would a lot of other things. I'm also very grateful to the Reverend Daisy Allen and Rabbis Jonathan Rubenstein and Linda Motzkin of Temple Sinai in Saratoga Springs, New York, and to the many others who have written me about their own celebrations.

Many thanks, of course, to my agent, Gloria Loomis, and to the many people at Simon & Schuster who were enthused by this book—most notably David Rosenthal, Annik La Farge, and Geoffrey Kloske. I am enormously grateful to Scott Savage, the editor of *Plain* magazine, who printed the covers for the first printing of this book on a century-old hand-fed press that he has converted to use solar power. He and Jeremiah Arn put in weeks of hard labor, very much in the spirit of this book—each copy is, in some sense, an original piece of handwork.

My family has been wonderfully understanding—my mother, Peggy McKibben, has embraced the spirit of Hundred Dollar Holidays more fully than anyone I know, each year creating small and beloved gifts for her children and grandchildren. My own daugh-

ter, Sophie, has taught me a lot about the season. And my wife, Sue Halpern, has been the most help of anyone—she worked with me to set up various church and synagogue programs, and also to think out the intellectual underpinnings of our modest campaign. And each year she gives me the Christmas present I anticipate most.

Finally, an important note on sources. When we started the Hundred Dollar Holidays program almost a decade ago, and I began my efforts to find how our Christmas celebrations developed their current form, there was very little good scholarship available. Happily, the mid-1990s saw the publication of two magnificent books. *Christmas in America,* by Penne Restad of the University of Texas, was issued by the Oxford University Press in 1995, and tells of Christmas on the frontier and in the cities, on the farm and in the slave quarters. And in 1996 Knopf issued Stephen Nissenbaum's *The Battle for Christmas,* which was deservedly nominated for a Pulitzer Prize, and which pays particularly close attention to the class and commercial needs which shaped the development of Christmas in America. My short history of our Christmas celebrations cribs from each of these books, and the reader who wants more information is encouraged to seek them out.

ABOUT THE AUTHOR

Bill McKibben's books include *Maybe One, The End of Nature, The Age of Missing Information, The Comforting Whirlwind,* and *Hope, Human and Wild.* He is a frequent contributor to a wide variety of publications, including *The New York Review of Books, Outside,* and *The New York Times.* A former staff writer for *The New Yorker,* he lives with his wife and daughter in the Adirondack Mountains of New York, where he is Sunday School superintendent of the local Methodist church.